The Canadian Rockies

CANADIAN ROCKIES SIGHTSEEING

Compliments of:

 Key West *Travel & Tours*

Toll-free:
UK: 08-08-101-4562
AU: 1-800-449-180
NZ: 0800-459-240
CANADA & USA: 1-888-632-3757
OTHER: 1-604-632-3757
www.keywesttours.ca

Summerthought

Banff, Canada

THE CANADIAN ROCKIES

Published by
Summerthought

Summerthought Publishing
PO Box 2309
Banff, AB T1L 1C1
Canada
www.summerthought.com

Design and production: Linda Petras
Printed in Canada by Friesens
Reprinted 2015

We gratefully acknowledge the financial support of the Alberta Multimedia Development Fund.

Alberta
Government

Library and Archives Canada Cataloguing in Publication

Hempstead, Andrew
The Canadian Rockies / Andrew Hempstead.

Book published with two different covers.

ISBN 978-1-926983-09-7 (Banff Springs cover).—ISBN 978-1-926983-10-3 (Bow Lake cover).

1. Rocky Mountains, Canadian (B.C. and Alta.)—Pictorial works. I. Title.

FC219.H4583 2013 971.10022'2 C2013-900724-5

CONTENTS

Sunrise over Cascade Mountain

Herbert Lake, Banff National Park

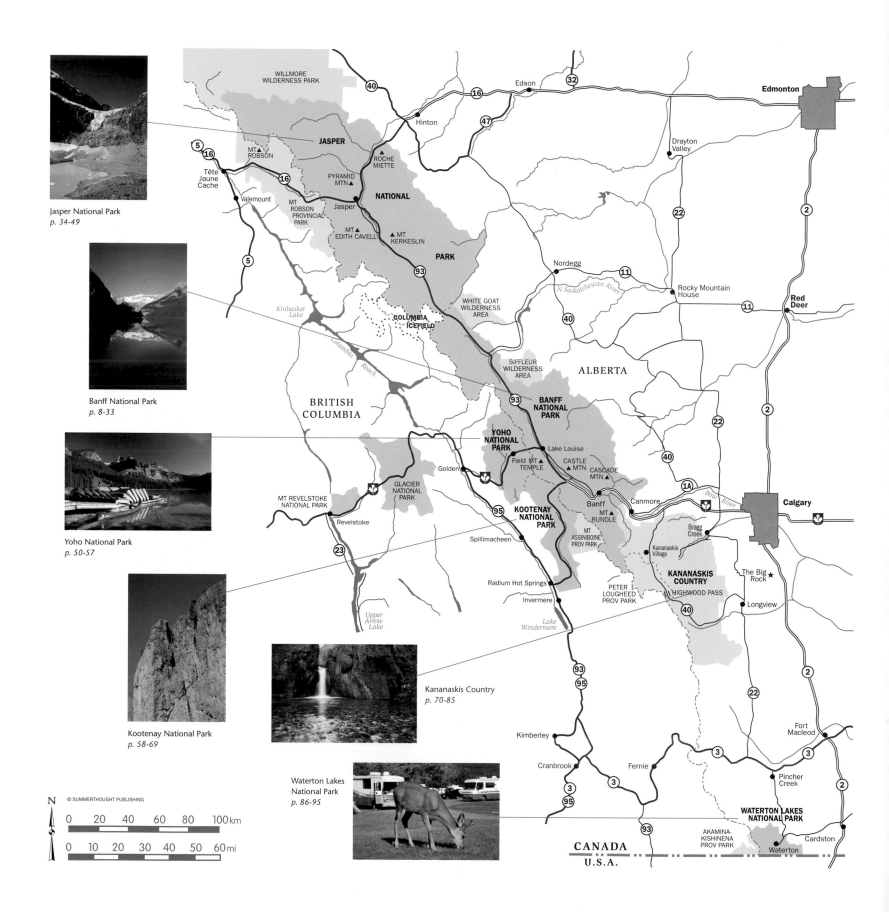

Jasper National Park
p. 34-49

Banff National Park
p. 8-33

Yoho National Park
p. 50-57

Kootenay National Park
p. 58-69

Kananaskis Country
p. 70-85

Waterton Lakes
National Park
p. 86-95

© SUMMERTHOUGHT PUBLISHING

N

0   20   40   60   80   100 km

0   10   20   30   40   50   60 mi

WILLMORE
WILDERNESS PARK

Edson

Edmonton

32

40

16

16

47

Hinton

22

Drayton
Valley

2

JASPER

MT
ROBSON

ROCHE
MIETTE

5

16

PYRAMID
MTN

NATIONAL

Tête
Jaune
Cache

16

Nordegg

11

22

Rocky Mountain
House

Red
Deer

Valemount

MT ROBSON
PROVINCIAL
PARK

Jasper

MT
EDITH CAVELL

MT KERKESLIN

93

PARK

5

11

WHITE GOAT
WILDERNESS
AREA

40

ALBERTA

BRITISH
COLUMBIA

Kinbasket
Lake

COLUMBIA
ICEFIELD

N Saskatchewan River

Columbia Reach

SIFFLEUR
WILDERNESS
AREA

93

BANFF
NATIONAL
PARK

22

2

YOHO
NATIONAL
PARK

Lake Louise

40

Golden

Field MT
TEMPLE

CASTLE
MTN

CASCADE
MTN

MT REVELSTOKE
NATIONAL PARK

GLACIER
NATIONAL
PARK

1A

Bow River

Calgary

Banff

Canmore

Revelstoke

KOOTENAY
NATIONAL
PARK

95

MT
RUNDLE

Bragg
Creek

23

Spillimacheen

MT
ASSINIBOINE
PROV PARK

Kananaskis
Village

KANANASKIS
COUNTRY

The Big
Rock

Radium Hot Springs

PETER
LOUGHEED
PROV PARK

HIGHWOOD PASS

Longview

Upper
Arrow
Lake

Invermere

Lake
Windermere

40

93

95

Kimberley

Cranbrook

Fernie

3

3

Pincher
Creek

2

Fort
Macleod

3

95

WATERTON LAKES
NATIONAL PARK

93

AKAMINA-
KISHINENA
PROV PARK

Cardston

CANADA

U.S.A.

Waterton

INTRODUCTION

Since we can't export the scenery we shall have to import the tourists.

—William Van Horne, 1886

Snowcapped peaks by the hundreds, glaciers and icefields, multihued lakes, rushing rivers, alpine meadows, and an abundance of wildlife make the **CANADIAN ROCKIES** a travel destination that is rivalled by few places in the world.

A northern extension of the Rocky Mountain chain running through the western United States, the Canadian Rockies extends north from the U.S. border for around 800 kilometres (500 miles). The spine of the Canadian Rockies is the Continental Divide, which runs the length of the range and separates the province of Alberta in the east from British Columbia in the west. Much of this wilderness is protected by contiguous parks, of which the best known is **BANFF NATIONAL PARK,** where the most familiar natural highlights—**LAKE LOUISE, MORAINE LAKE,** and **PEYTO LAKE**—are all very accessible. To the north, **JASPER NATIONAL PARK** is bigger and wilder, but it's still just a short ride on an oversized Ice Explorer bus up and onto the magnificent **COLUMBIA ICEFIELD.** Two more national parks, **KOOTENAY** and **YOHO,** lie west of Banff in British Columbia. The mountainous landscape they protect is no less impressive than Banff, especially the area around **LAKE O'HARA** and **EMERALD LAKE.** Together, these four national parks—along with adjoining provincial parks—make up a complex geological and natural area that has been declared a **WORLD HERITAGE SITE** by the United Nations Educational, Scientific, and Cultural Organization (UNESCO). Within **KANANASKIS COUNTRY,** an area south of **CANMORE** developed as a multiuse

Lake O'Hara

recreation area, are facilities for all interests, as well as plenty of wilderness where escaping the crowds is easy. In southern Alberta, **WATERTON LAKES NATIONAL PARK** lacks the crowds of its northern counterparts, yet packs a lot of scenery into mountainous terrain.

The first visitors to the Canadian Rockies were native people, who regarded the "Shining Mountains" as a sacred place. In the 1880s, a rail line was built across the mountains, with grand resorts such as the Banff Springs Hotel developed as a way of luring tourists looking for a wilderness experience while enjoying luxurious accommodations. While natural beauty is the main selling point of the Canadian Rockies, the growth of towns as tourist resorts has created an ideal destination for all interests and budgets. One visitor may spend their day walking the fairways of one of the world's most scenic golf courses, taking a gondola to a mountain peak, soaking away their cares in a European-style spa, and then dining in a fine French restaurant before retiring to a bed covered in a goose-down duvet. Another visitor may strike out early on foot for a remote alpine lake, go whitewater rafting in the afternoon, and then return to pitch a tent and sit around a campfire watching dinner grill itself to perfection. All the while, an abundance of wildlife makes itself known in the most unexpected places— an elk grazing on the golf course, deer making themselves at home within residential areas, or a bear feasting on dandelions as you ride overhead on a gondola.

BANFF NATIONAL PARK

No scene has ever given me an equal impression of inspiring solitude and rugged grandeur.

—Walter Wilcox, 1899

This 6,641-square-kilometre (2,564-square-mile) national park encompasses some of the world's most magnificent scenery. The snowcapped peaks of the Rocky Mountains form a spectacular backdrop for glacial lakes, fast-flowing rivers, and endless forests. Deer, moose, elk, mountain goats, bighorn sheep, black and grizzly bears, wolves, and cougars inhabit the park's vast wilderness, while the human species is concentrated in the picture-postcard **TOWN OF BANFF** and the **VILLAGE OF LAKE LOUISE**—two of North America's most famous vacation destinations. One of the park's greatest drawing cards is the accessibility of its natural wonders. Most highlights are close to the road system. But adventurous visitors can follow an excellent system of hiking trails to alpine lakes, along glacial valleys, and to spectacular viewpoints where crowds are scarce and human impact is minimal.

Many visitors planning a trip to the national park don't realize that the town of Banff is a bustling commercial centre within the park itself. The town's location is magnificent. It is spread out along the **BOW RIVER,** extending to the lower slopes of **SULPHUR MOUNTAIN** to the south and **TUNNEL MOUNTAIN** to the east. In one direction is the towering face of **MOUNT RUNDLE,** and in the other, framed by the buildings along Banff Avenue, is **CASCADE MOUNTAIN.** Hotels and motels line the north end of **BANFF AVENUE,** while a profusion of shops, boutiques, cafes, and restaurants hugs

the south end. Some people are happy walking through this scenic town and shopping in a truly unique setting; those more interested in some peace and quiet can easily slip into pristine wilderness just a five-minute walk from town. A short drive north, **LAKE LOUISE,** which is regarded as one of the seven natural wonders of the world, is rivalled for sheer beauty only by **MORAINE LAKE,** just down the road. Just north of Lake Louise, the **ICEFIELDS PARKWAY** begins its spectacular course alongside the Continental Divide to Jasper National Park. Highlights along the way include **BOW LAKE** and **PEYTO LAKE,** both showing off the beautiful turquoise water that the Canadian Rockies are known for.

Although the valleys of the Canadian Rockies became ice free nearly 8,000 years ago and native people periodically have hunted in the area since that time, the story of Banff National Park really began with the arrival of the railroad to the area in the 1880s. Word of soothing hot springs soon got out, and the government encouraged visitors to the **CAVE AND BASIN** as an ongoing source of revenue to support the new railway. A reserve was established around the springs and two years later, in 1887, the reserve was expanded and renamed Rocky Mountains Park. It was primarily a business enterprise centred on the unique springs and catering to wealthy patrons of the railway, but has evolved into Banff National Park, one of the world's most famous and most visited parks.

Mount Chephren

Indian paintbrush (opposite)

Town of Banff
A classic winter evening view looking north along Banff Avenue to Cascade Mountain. This famous street is the town of Banff's main thoroughfare. Lined with shops and restaurants, it is the centerpiece of a bustling town of 8,000 residents, many of whom work in tourism or industries related to serving the four million visitors that arrive annually.

Cascade Ponds
Close to the town, this day use area has Mount Rundle as a backdrop. Lakeside tables make it an ideal place for a summer picnic, while the brave take to the chilly water for a quick swim.

The Fairmont Banff Springs (opposite)
There can be few things more evocative of the human history of the Canadian Rockies than strolling through the grand hallways of The Fairmont Banff Springs, one of the world's most famous mountain resorts.

Lake Minnewanka
In winter, snow covers the road to Lake Minnewanka, while in summer the lake provides the opportunity for a myriad of water sports ranging from boat tours to fishing, and even scuba diving (opposite).

Sunrise over Mount Rundle
Vermilion Lakes is a favourite spot to watch
the sun rise over Mount Rundle, which is the
dominant peak to the south of the town of Banff.

Vermilion Lakes
On the edge of town, three shallow lakes and extensive wetlands provide a home for wildlife such as elk, deer, and bears, as well as over 200 species of birds.

Bugling elk (opposite)
Elk are common throughout the Canadian Rockies, but are especially prolific around the towns of Banff and Jasper. Each fall, the mature males define their territory and attract females by "bugling."

Osprey
Ospreys nest high up on dead trees or telephone poles, always overlooking water, where they feed on fish.

Castle Mountain (opposite)
Thrusting high out of the Bow Valley, this distinctive peak is difficult to miss on the drive between Banff and Lake Louise. It is named for its castle-like appearance, which has been accentuated by wind and water erosion.

Lake Louise
Deemed by many to be one of the most beautiful lakes on Earth, the jewel-like waters of Lake Louise draw millions of visitors annually to the Canadian Rockies.

Winter at Lake Louise
Lake Louise in winter is a magical place. Skaters young and old glide across the frozen lake, families enjoy sleigh rides, and skiers and boarders take to the slopes of one of Canada's finest ski resorts.

Moraine Lake (above and opposite)
"No scene has ever given me an equal impression of inspiring solitude and rugged grandeur" wrote explorer Walter Wilcox after becoming the first white man to lay eyes on Moraine Lake. These words, and those of many who followed, guaranteed the lake's popularity as one of the most beautiful places in the Canadian Rockies.

Herbert Lake

Herbert Lake at sunrise epitomizes the ultimate Canadian Rockies experience for photographers looking to escape the hustle and bustle of nearby Lake Louise. It also marks the first stop for northbound travellers on the Icefields Parkway, a scenic mountain drive linking Banff and Jasper national parks.

Crowfoot Glacier
The aptly named Crowfoot Glacier is easily recognized from the Icefields Parkway.
Sitting atop Crowfoot Mountain, its glacial "claws" cling to steep slopes above the highway.
The retreat of this glacier has been dramatic—only 70 years ago, it extended almost to the valley floor.

Fall colours (opposite)
In September, the leaves of trembling aspen turn brilliant shades of yellow and orange.
Stands of aspen are present in valleys throughout the Canadian Rockies, including
at lower elevations along the Icefields Parkway.

Bow Lake
Beautiful Bow Lake stretches from the Icefields Parkway to Crowfoot Mountain and the distant Crowfoot Glacier.

North Saskatchewan River
The North Saskatchewan River flows eastward from Banff National Park through the Alberta capital

Peyto Lake
Reputedly a favourite camping spot for iconic mountain man "Wild" Bill Peyto, the water of this lake changes colour throughout the year as glacial runoff increases and decreases. From this lookout, the panorama is particularly enchanting, as views extend seemingly forever down the Mistaya Valley.

JASPER NATIONAL PARK

All in our little party agreed, it was the finest view any of us had beheld in the Rockies.

—Mary Schäffer, 1908

Snowcapped peaks, vast icefields, beautiful glacial lakes, soothing hot springs, thundering rivers, and the most extensive backcountry trail system of any Canadian national park make Jasper a stunning counterpart to its sister park, Banff.

Within this 10,900-square-kilometre (4,208-square-mile) park, many spectacular natural landmarks can be admired from the **ICEFIELDS PARKWAY,** which connects Jasper with Lake Louise, in Banff National Park. None are more spectacular than the **COLUMBIA ICEFIELD,** which covers approximately 325 square kilometres (125 square miles) and is up to 400 metres (1,300 feet) deep—it's the most extensive icefield in the Rocky Mountains. Those not content with simply admiring this remnant of the last ice age can jump aboard a big-wheeled **ICE EXPLORER** and get up close and personal with the ancient ice flow. At the north end of the Icefields Parkway is the **TOWN OF JASPER,** the park's main service centre. With half the population of Banff, its setting— at the confluence of the Athabasca and Miette Rivers, surrounded by rugged, snowcapped peaks—is a little less dramatic, though still beautiful. But the town is also less commercialised than Banff and its streets quieter—a major plus for those looking to get away from it all. The town and its many lodgings, including the famous **JASPER PARK LODGE,** make an ideal base for exploring the north end of the park. One of the busiest routes— and with good reason—leads past the depths of **MALIGNE CANYON** to gemlike **MALIGNE LAKE,** where glacial silt suspended in the lake's water produces amazing emerald, turquoise, and amethyst colours. Other roads lead to the base of towering **MOUNT EDITH CAVELL,** to the soothing oasis of **MIETTE HOT SPRINGS,** and east alongside a string of shallow lakes toward the provincial capital of Edmonton.

The first white man to enter what is now Jasper National Park was David Thompson, one of Canada's greatest explorers. Thompson travelled up the Athabasca River Valley in the winter of 1810-11 and made the first recorded crossing of the Athabasca Pass. Along the way, he established the small supply post of Henry's House near what is now the town of Jasper. In the ensuing years, other trading posts were built along the Athabasca River, including one that became known as Jasper's House, for the clerk Jasper Hawse. In 1907, aware that the coming of the railway would mean an influx of settlers, the federal government set aside 5,000 square miles as Jasper Forest Park. In 1911, a construction camp was established for the Grand Trunk Pacific Railway near the present site of downtown Jasper. When the line was completed, visitors flocked into the remote mountain settlement, and its future was assured.

Adjacent to Jasper is British Columbia's **MOUNT ROBSON PROVINCIAL PARK,** created to protect a wilderness of forested valleys, fast-flowing rivers, and rugged mountain peaks permanently blanketed in snow and ice. Towering over the park's western entrance is magnificent 3,954-metre (12,972-foot) **MOUNT ROBSON,** the highest peak in the Canadian Rockies.

Two Brothers totem pole

Maligne Lake (opposite)

Lac Beauvert
Even the name augurs well—Beauvert (French for "beautiful"). The Fairmont Jasper Park Lodge spreads around the shore of this turquoise lake. The resort's stunning outlook, historic ambience, and wide range of amenities have been enchanting guests from around the world since 1922.

Angel Glacier

Clinging to the face of Mount Edith Cavell, this glacier has receded greatly in the last 100 years—the angel's "wings" are no longer and adjacent Ghost Glacier collapsed in 2012. A short hiking trail leads to the small iceberg-filled lake pictured, while another leads past this viewpoint on the way to Cavell Meadows.

Mount Edith Cavell (opposite)

Tucked away below Cavell Road—and not signposted—is Cavell Lake, a small body of water that on a calm morning perfectly frames 3,363-metre (11,033-foot) Mount Edith Cavell. The peak is named for an heroic English nurse who helped allied soldiers caught behind enemy lines during World War I.

Maligne Canyon
The power of water is at its most dramatic at Maligne Canyon, where it has carved a gorge just two metres (six feet) wide and up to 50 metres (160 feet) deep into limestone bedrock. Geologists surmise that sections of the canyon are part of a cave network, some of which have collapsed.

Jasper Lake (opposite)
In a cycle that repeats itself each year, sand-like glacial sediment is washed downstream and settles on the bed of Jasper Lake. As the level of the lake drops each fall, the sand is exposed and prevailing westerly winds blow the sand into dunes along the highway.

Maligne Lake

Maligne Lake is the largest natural lake in the Canadian Rockies. Taking a tour boat to Spirit Island (right) is popular with visitors, while other activities include renting a canoe from the historic boathouse (opposite) and hiking along the shore to a lookout with sweeping lake views. One of the most serene times to visit Maligne Lake is at dawn (following pages).

Grizzly bear
The largest and most feared predator in the Canadian Rockies is the grizzly bear. Although it is estimated that the region is home to around 800 grizzlies, these magnificent mammals spend most of their lives in the remote backcountry, purposely avoiding contact with humans.

Sunwapta Falls (opposite)
This torrent of cold water tumbles into a deep gorge formed during the last ice age when a glacier retreated across a U-shaped valley left by a much larger glacier. The effect was a "hanging valley," and the falls as they exist today.

Mount Athabasca
One of many imposing peaks passed by those driving along the Icefields Parkway is Mount Athabasca, a glaciated mountain that towers above the Columbia Icefield. On warmer days, streams of glacial meltwater flow from its slopes through the surrounding moon-like landscape.

Columbia Icefield
Mostly hidden from the Icefields Parkway, the Columbia Icefield is surrounded by snowcapped peaks along the top of the Continental Divide. The best way to experience this intriguing landscape is aboard an Ice Explorer, an oversized bus developed especially for glacial travel.

YOHO NATIONAL PARK

Emerald Lake is a happy hunting ground for the traveller who has not the time or experience for wandering far from the railroad.

—J Monroe Thorington, 1925

Yoho, a Cree word of amazement, is a fitting name for this 1,313-square-kilometre (507-square-mile) park on the **BRITISH COLUMBIA** side of the Canadian Rockies immediately west of Banff National Park. Yoho is the smallest of the four contiguous Canadian Rockies national parks, but its wild and rugged landscape holds spectacular waterfalls, extensive icefields, a lake to rival those in Banff, fast-flowing glacial rivers, and one of the world's most intriguing fossil beds. In addition, you'll find some of the finest day hiking in all of Canada on the park's 300-kilometre (186-mile) trail system.

The first Europeans to explore the valley of the **KICKING HORSE RIVER** were members of the 1858 Palliser Expedition, which set out to survey the west and report back to the British government on its suitability for settlement. The unfortunate expedition geologist, Dr. James Hector, inadvertently gave the Kicking Horse River its name. While walking his horse over rough ground, he was kicked unconscious and took two hours to come to, by which time, so the story goes, other members of his party had begun digging his grave. The Canadian Pacific Railway (CPR) completed a railbed over the Kicking Horse Pass from the prairies in 1884, but its grade on the west side of the pass was terribly steep. In 1909, after dozens of wrecks and derailments, the CPR rerouted the steepest section of the line through the man-made **SPIRAL TUNNELS,** which can be viewed from a roadside viewpoint.

While most early visitors arrived by rail, it is the modern day Trans-Canada Highway that provides today's access. This route bisects the park on its run between Lake Louise (Alberta) and Golden (British Columbia), crossing Kicking Horse Pass and descending quickly to the valley of the Kicking Horse River, which is fed by the Wapta and Waputik icefields. Here, the **VILLAGE OF FIELD** lies in the shadow of Mt. Stephen and side roads lead to two major attractions. **TAKAKKAW FALLS,** Canada's second highest waterfall, plunges magnificently into the Yoho Valley, while beautiful **EMERALD LAKE** is nestled in a verdant forested bowl seemingly far removed from the outside world.

LAKE O'HARA and its surrounds are one of the most beautiful destinations in all of the Canadian Rockies, especially in fall, when needles of larch trees turn a brilliant golden colour. An upscale backcountry lodge, an alpine hut, and a campground provide the opportunity for visitors to Lake O'Hara to extend their stay beyond a single day. Less accessible in Yoho is the **BURGESS SHALE,** protected site of the most important fossils found anywhere in the Canadian Rockies. These are the animals for which this park is best known—fossilized remains of creatures found nowhere else on earth and dated at more than 500 million years old. They create great interest for the role their remains have played in our understanding of life on earth in prehistoric times.

Takakkaw Falls

Yoho River (opposite)

Lake O'Hara
Accessible only on foot or by shuttle bus, Lake O'Hara is a popular spot for day hiking and overnight trips. Experienced hikers tackle the Alpine Circuit for stunning views of the lake (opposite) while in fall, the larch of Opabin Plateau (above) turn a delightful golden colour.

Emerald Lake (previous pages)
Emerald Lake is a true gem. Its glowing turquoise waters are surrounded by towering peaks while sprawling along the shoreline is Emerald Lake Lodge, artfully combining rustic charm with upscale elegance.

Village of Field

Originally a railway construction camp, the village of Field (above) is a cluster of simple yet colourful homes sandwiched between lofty peaks and the tumbling glacial waters of the Kicking Horse River. Beside the highway is the Park Visitor Centre and a turquoise-coloured pond (opposite). Around 200 people, mostly park and railway workers, call Field home.

KOOTENAY NATIONAL PARK AND THE COLUMBIA VALLEY

If one halts by chance anywhere on a mountain pass, all sorts of thrilling things are going on around.

—Arthur Philemon Coleman, 1902

Kootenay may not have the famous resort towns of Banff and Jasper, but what it has it does well: vast areas of wilderness, abundant wildlife, and a network of hiking trails that are suited to all levels of fitness. **HIGHWAY 93,** extending for 94 kilometres (58 miles) through the park, provides access to natural attractions like **MARBLE CANYON** and the **PAINT POTS,** as well as phenomena such as **RADIUM HOT SPRINGS,** which have been tweaked for human enjoyment. Also along the route are easy interpretive hikes, scenic viewpoints, hot springs, picnic areas, and roadside interpretive exhibits.

Shaped like a lightning bolt, this 1,406-square-kilometre (542-square-mile) park lies on the **BRITISH COLUMBIA** side of the Canadian Rockies, protecting the upper headwaters of the **VERMILION** and **KOOTENAY RIVERS.** The park's northern section is bordered by Banff National Park and Mount Assiniboine Provincial Park to the east and Yoho National Park to the north. As elsewhere in the Canadian Rockies, the geology of the park is complex. Over the last 70 million years, these mountains have been pushed upward—folded and faulted along the way—by massive forces deep beneath the earth's surface. They've also been subject to erosion that entire time, particularly during the ice ages, when glaciers carved U-shaped valleys and high cirques into the landscape. These features, along with glacial lakes and the remnants of the glaciers themselves, are readily visible in the park today. The hillsides scarred from wildfires that swept

through the park in 2001 and 2003 will be obvious from the highway, but the trail along Marble Canyon is the best place to see the natural regeneration process at work.

Although their traditional home was along the river valley to the south, the indigenous Kootenay people regularly came to this area to enjoy the hot springs. Construction of the Banff-Windermere Road began in 1911, but with three mountain ranges to negotiate and deep, fast-flowing rivers to cross, the money ran out after completion of only 22 kilometres (13.6 miles). To get the highway project going again, the provincial government agreed to hand over an eight-kilometre-wide (five-mile-wide) section of land along both sides of the proposed highway to the federal government. In return, the government agreed to finance completion of the highway. Originally called the Highway Park, the land became known as Kootenay National Park in 1920. The highway was finally completed in 1922, and the official ribbon-cutting ceremony was held at Kootenay Crossing in 1923; a plaque marks the spot.

The highway south from Kootenay National Park passes through the **COLUMBIA VALLEY,** where large lakes and hot summer temperatures are major attractions for Albertans, many of whom own vacation homes in the valley. For visitors driving north from the United States, Highway 93 through the Columbia Valley is the most direct route to Banff and Jasper.

Fireweed

Vermilion River (opposite)

Kootenay wildfires

In 2001, and then again in 2003, wildfires swept through Kootenay National Park,
roared up mountainsides, and jumped over Highway 93 in numerous places.
The effects of fire can still be seen along the highway, and is accentuated by snow (opposite).

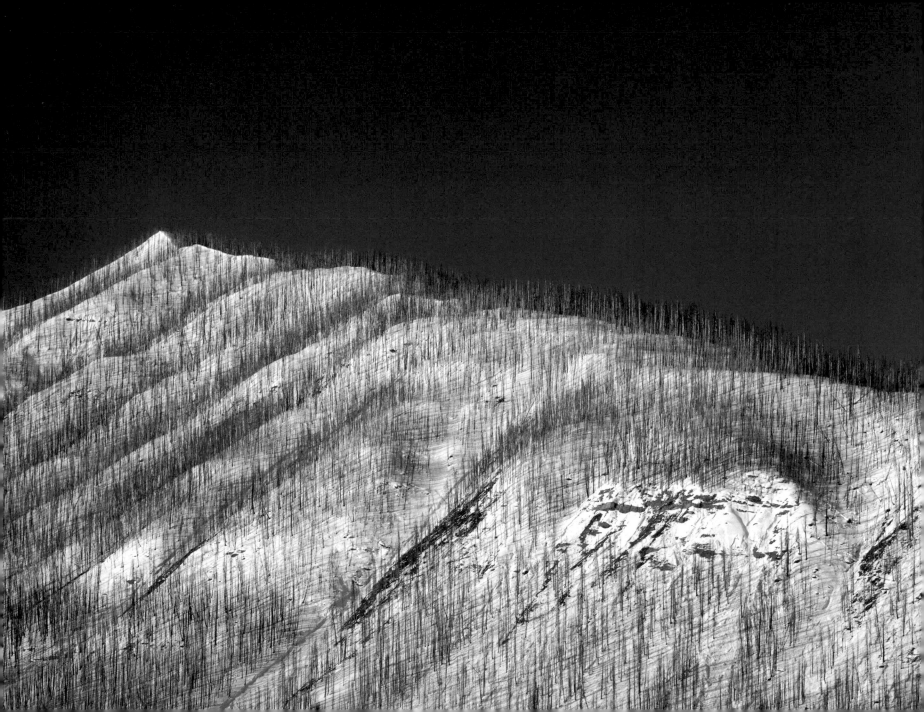

Marble Canyon
Over thousands of years, the rushing waters of Tokumm Creek have carved a deep gorge through limestone bedrock to create Marble Canyon. A walking trail follows the rim through a forest destroyed by a wildfire in 2003.

Numa Falls
As morning dawns, rays of sunlight flood into Vermilion Canyon, creating intriguing light patterns on the water flowing over Numa Falls.

Fireweed
Fireweed, which thrives after wildfires, is common throughout the valleys of Kootenay National Park. Its distinctive pink flowers are at their peak in mid-August each year.

Wolf (opposite)
Wolf numbers in the Canadian Rockies have increased greatly over the last two decades. This curious young male was photographed in a flower-filled meadow beside the Vermilion River.

Paint Pots

These colourful ochre beds were of special cultural significance to the First Nations peoples, who collected the red earth to use for painting their bodies, tepees, and clothes. Reached by a short walk from Highway 93, the "paint pots" are comprised of three mineral springs, each with a rim of iron that has built up over time.

Redwall Fault
At the top of Sinclair Canyon, the
highway passes below these dramatic
cliffs of iron-rich rock. They are
part of the Redwall Fault, created
by tectonic forces originating deep
below the Earth's surface. It is these
same forces that heat the water
at nearby Radium Hot Springs.

Columbia Valley
Dominated by Lake Windermere (pictured), this valley west of Kootenay National Park attracts hordes of outdoor enthusiasts throughout summer.

Rosen Lake (opposite)
At the south end of the Canadian Rockies, Rosen is one of many lakes nestled in the shadow of the Lizard Range. This photo was taken at dusk on an evening when smoke from a nearby wildfire filled the air.

KANANASKIS COUNTRY AND CANMORE

Never has any mountain summit given me such an impression of crushingly sublime.

—Dr. August Eggers, 1903

Pronounced exactly as it reads, this recreational playground lies adjacent to Banff National Park and is handy for Calgarians who flock west to revel in a diverse range of outdoor activities, or simply to do nothing at all. Throughout Kananaskis Country, wildlife is abundant and opportunities for observation of larger mammals are superb. Along with scenery that rivals nearby national parks, facilities are top-notch—eight provincial parks, an alpine resort developed for the 1988 Winter Olympic Games, world-class golfing, 1,300 kilometres (800 miles) of hiking and biking trails, 30 lakes stocked annually with more than 150,000 fish, horseback riding, over 1,000 campsites, lodging for the disabled, and even a self-contained resort village.

Kananaskis Country holds two distinct ecosystems: the high peaks of the Continental Divide to the west and the lower, rolling foothills to the east. The glacier-carved **KANANASKIS VALLEY** separates the two. Much of Kananaskis Country occupies a transition zone between foothills and mountains, and as a result it harbours a wide variety of plant and animal species. One of the most accessible alpine areas in the Canadian Rockies is the **HIGHWOOD PASS,** where forget-me-nots, Indian paintbrush, and western anemone bloom during the short summer season. These hills, valleys, and forests are home to an abundance of wildlife, including large populations of moose, mule deer, white-

tailed deer, elk, black bear, bighorn sheep, and mountain goat. Also present, but less likely to be seen, are grizzly bears and cougars.

Little known outside of Alberta, Kananaskis Country was born from Alberta's oil boom in the 1970s. During this period, oil revenues collected by the provincial government were channelled into various projects aimed at improving the lifestyle of Albertans, one of which was the development of the Kananaskis region into a four-season recreation area.

In a little over three decades, **CANMORE,** on the northern edge of Kananaskis Country and a short drive from Banff National Park, has transformed itself from a coal-mining town to a hotbed of recreational pursuits with a charming downtown core. The surrounding wilderness provides Canmore's best recreation opportunities. Hiking is excellent on trails that lace the valley and mountainside slopes, with many high viewpoints easily reached. Flowing though town, the **BOW RIVER** offers great fishing, kayaking, and rafting; golfers flock to three scenic courses; and nearby Mount Yamnuska has become the most developed rock-climbing site in the Canadian Rockies. Canmore also hosted the Nordic events of the 1988 Winter Olympic Games and is home to the Alpine Club of Canada.

**Welcome to
Kananaskis Country**

Highway 40 through the Kananaskis Valley (opposite)

Barrier Lake
Prairie View trail climbs from the valley floor to a lofty viewpoint, from where
Barrier Lake and the Kananaskis Valley are laid out below in all their glory.

Spray Lake (opposite)
This 18-kilometre-long (11-mile) man-made reservoir is part of a hydroelectric
development that supplies power to Canmore. It is a busy recreational spot with
camping, fishing, boating, and nearby hiking all popular summer activities.

Moose
One of the best places to see moose in all of the Canadian Rockies is Peter Lougheed Provincial Park, at the south end of Kananaskis Valley. Look for them along the valley floor and in shallow lakes.

Bighorn sheep
Bighorn sheep are named for their impressive curled horns, which can weigh up to 14 kilograms (30 pounds). They are widespread throughout the Canadian Rockies, but tend to congregate in certain spots, such as along Highway 546 west of Turner Valley.

Mud Lake

Aptly named Mud Lake may not have the famous blue and green hues of better known lakes in the
Canadian Rockies, but on a calm day the view across its muddy waters is one of utter tranquility.

Kananaskis Country Golf Course
Renowned golf course architect
Robert Trent Jones Sr., who
designed the 36-hole Kananaskis
Country Golf Course, described
the site as "the best spot I have
ever seen for a golf course."

Fall colours (opposite)
Through September, groves of
aspen trees scattered through
Kananaskis Country turn brilliant
shades of yellow and orange.
This photo was taken in late
September beside Barrier Lake.

Sheep Falls
West of Turner Valley, the Sheep River tumbles over this small cascade on its way east to the Bow River.
The falls are within Sheep River Provincial Park, designated to protect year round habitat of bighorn sheep.

Cat Creek Falls
More remote than Sheep Falls,
traffic noise from the highway
quickly abates as the trail to Cat
Creek descends from a dry ridge into
a cool gully. The photogenic falls
mark the end of the trail, and a good
place to rest with a picnic lunch.

Canmore Hoodoos

These intriguing rock formations stand guard over Canmore from the north side of the Trans-Canada Highway. They have been created by erosion, as wind, water, and snow has worn down softer surrounding sedimentary material. Hoodoos are also found in Banff and Yoho National Parks.

Ha Ling and Mt. Lawrence Grassi (opposite)

These two mountains, rising majestically above the town of Canmore, have watched over three decades of growth in the Bow Valley. One constant is the surrounding wilderness that remains just that—a recreational year-round playground for outdoor enthusiasts from around the world.

Three Sisters
Dominating the skyline south of Canmore, the Three Sisters were originally
named the Three Nuns in 1883 for their resemblance to praying nuns.

Canmore Nordic Centre
Built for the 1988 Winter Olympic Games, the Canmore Nordic Centre proudly hosts international cross-country skiing and biathlon events every winter. The trails are also open for the public to enjoy.

WATERTON LAKES NATIONAL PARK

This is what I have seen in my dreams, this is the country for me.

—George "Kootenai" Brown, 1865

The old cliche that good things come in small packages couldn't be a truer description of 526-square-kilometre (203-square-mile) Waterton Lakes National Park, separated only by an international border from Glacier National Park in Montana. The dramatic mountain splendour, a chain of deep glacial lakes, large and diverse populations of wildlife, an unbelievable variety of day hikes, a memorable scenic boat tour, and a charming lakeside village make this park a gem that shouldn't be missed on any trip to the Canadian Rockies.

The drive into Waterton Lakes is almost as scenic as the park itself. From whichever direction you arrive, the transition from prairie to mountains is abrupt. Perched along the shore of **UPPER WATERTON LAKE** and watched over by the grand **PRINCE OF WALES HOTEL, WATERTON VILLAGE** oozes mountain charm. Running parallel to the lake, the tree-lined main street holds a pleasing mix of businesses—boutiques and souvenir shops, restaurants with patios, a camping and outdoor store, and an old-fashioned ice cream parlour. Beyond the main street are a number of comfortable lodgings to suit all budgets, a campground within walking distance of all services, and a few rows of simple bungalows that provide a home for residents. The most popular activity in Waterton is to take a **BOAT TOUR** across the international border to Montana. Hiking is another popular activity for visitors. Popular trails lead past Bertha Falls to **BERTHA**

LAKE, to the top of the Bear's Hump for sweeping valley views, and along the shore of Upper Waterton Lake. Access to the heart of the park is along two narrow, winding roads—one ending at the turquoise expanse of **CAMERON LAKE**, the other at intriguing **RED ROCK CANYON.** If you're looking for wildlife, Waterton Lakcs will exceed your expectations. Mule deer and bighorn sheep are common within the village, while both black and grizzly bears are often sighted along park roads.

Although there is evidence that native people camped in what is now the park up to 8,000 years ago, the first permanent settler was John "Kootenai" Brown, who built a cabin by Upper Waterton Lake in 1869. Brown was employed as a warden for the original Forest Reserve, and then in 1911, when the area was declared a national park, he was appointed its superintendent. Even without a rail link—which propelled Banff and Jasper into world-renown as tourist destinations—Waterton Lakes soon became a popular summer retreat with a hotel, a restaurant, boat tours across the border to Montana, and a dance hall. In 1932, the Canadian and U.S. governments agreed to establish Waterton-Glacier International Peace Park, the world's first such park. In 1979, UNESCO declared **WATERTON-GLACIER INTERNATIONAL PEACE PARK** a biosphere reserve. In 1995 the park's importance was further recognized when UNESCO declared a World Heritage Site.

MV *International,*
Upper Waterton Lake

Upper Waterton Lake (opposite)

Prairies to peaks
Although the smallest of Canada's mountain national parks, Waterton Lakes more than makes up for
its diminutive size with a diverse range of landscapes. This is especially apparent to those driving along
the Red Rock Canyon Parkway, where prairies extend all the way to steep rocky mountainsides.

Waterton Lakes (previous pages)
The three interconnected Waterton Lakes extend into Montana's Glacier National Park.
In 1932, the two parks joined to become the world's first International Peace Park.

Red Rock Canyon
At the end of the Red Rock Canyon Parkway, erosion has carved a shallow

Western heritage
Beyond the boundaries of Waterton Lakes National Park, some of
North America's finest ranch land extends east to the Canadian prairies.

Maskinonge wetlands
The park access road bisects the extensive Maskinonge wetlands, which are
rich in plant-life and home to abundant bird species including trumpeter swans

Accessible wildlife
Mule deer are a common sight in Waterton Village. They can be seen grazing on grass in the campground (pictured), along the waterfront, and even in the yards of local residents.

Prince of Wales Hotel (opposite)
In the tradition of railway hotels in Banff and Jasper, Waterton's grandiose Prince of Wales Hotel opened in 1927. Unlike its more famous neighbours, the Prince of Wales had no railway link, but instead was operated by the Great Northern Railway as part of a hotel chain in Glacier National Park.

INDEX